Silhouette of a Songbird

Elizabeth Shane

Sunesis Ministries Ltd

Published by Sunesis Ministries Ltd. For more information about Sunesis Ministries Ltd, please visit:

www.stuartpattico.com

ISBN: 978-1-9163874-2-3

CONTENTS

ACKNOWLEDGEMENTS

I would like to thank my beautiful fairy godmother and drama teacher, Lucinda, for your friendship and encouragement to start writing, and for giving me the courage to open my heart, providing a safe space to express my deepest, darkest thoughts through the power of words. Without your continuous faith in me, I would never have had the opportunity to know my own potential of using poetry as a way of helping me survive the storm.

Thank you to my counsellor, Eileen, for your constant support and being there through my emotional rollercoaster of a journey. You have held my fears, witnessed my struggles, and never lost hope I would find my way out of the darkness.

I would also like to thank my singing and drama teachers, Elaine, Christine and Emma, for seeing the light shine when I couldn't; giving me the confidence to find my voice and be myself, which I've often been too scared to do.

Thank you to Katherine for guiding me through the editing process and giving life to my poems, as well as your wonderful suggestion for the title of this book.

Thank you to Lilly and Stuart for all their help making this book become reality.

Lastly, I would like to thank my husband Dave and son, Noah, not only for giving me the time and space to write, but for your unwavering love and never giving up on me.

Sometimes you just need to listen quietly to the ocean and let it speak to you.

EMPTY VESSEL

Suffocated into silence, no sound, no voice, sent to the
shadows of non-existence

The world didn't rejoice on the day of birth. Another burden
for the table, another face to blame

No reason to smile, no reason to celebrate, no reason to love,
no reason to be

Someone new to scare, someone new to shame, someone new
to use, someone new to the darkness

Razorblade words that rip and shred. The heart that closes
with no way in. Hands that remove the innocence of life

The tangled, forbidden fruits of the forest, no desire to taste,
no wish to enter

The light keeps fading, the star out of reach, reflections
shimmer false hope

No way out of the forest

Silent cries, an abandoned vessel running empty, sailing to a
place to forget

A vacant heart waiting to be filled. A cry waiting to be heard, a
body waiting for warmth

The wings ready to fly away and start again, a new sound, a
new voice, a new chance, a new chapter, a new
tomorrow

WALLPAPER

Sometimes her head was just a blank empty box staring into space. Sitting for hours staring at nothing or at the wall. Without knowing why, it seemed quite comforting looking at the familiar spot each time. Almost like a shield to hide the eyes from what was going on. She got used to having a vacant gaze, taking in a meaningless day. The wallpaper was the only map owned and could trace with her eyes, losing herself in a flower of patterns. She always wished there could be flowers so she could immerse herself forever in a forest full of colour.

A MIRROR OF MEMORIES

Is it time?

Am I ready to look

In a mirror of memories?

Which face will I see

When I search deep inside?

Yours?

Mine?

Who will get there first

In a mirror of memories?

For it surely can't lie.

How will I know what face to believe

When I look for the truth in the untold eye?

The one from the day, or the dreams from the night?

So many stories with ribbons still tied

Pick one box to open

Slowly at first

Fragile glass can shatter in two

Leaving a reflection still left to choose,

Should I wish to wipe clean the fuzzy haze

In a mirror of memories.

THE SIMPLE STONE

The simple stone. That's all it should be. But it's not. It's cold. It's unforgiving. It tries to hide a layer of dark shadows beneath the stark, solid surface, sugar coated with words. They don't say what the heart finds scared to set free. There is no softness, no forgiveness, no way back, no way of ever knowing. The blank emptiness can never have enough space to fill it with words that struggle with conflict and shame.

Words that hate. Words that blame. Words that are yet set free of pain. They are not there on the stone. How can they be? It could never be there for the world to see. The words want to scream out loud. Why? Why leave without knowing the truth? Why leave without freeing the light underneath the darkness? Why leave without saying sorry? Why leave without saying goodbye? Why can't the stone radiate any warmth so the words can be softer and kind?

The heart doesn't want the stone to stand alone, with an empty message put there for show. Instead, the words want to be loving, gentle and caring and feel safe to share the guilt they are wearing. They long to hold the stone tight and take it with them. But the weight from the stone would be too much to carry, so maybe the heart needs to leave it right there.

For within the core, only when it can see to accept the pain from the stone and be set free, the heart can look and take back the good and leave the bad memories alone and say goodbye to the simple stone.

A HAT

A hat. Not fancy, not feathered, not woolly, just a simple black hat. Almost a cold hat, a heartless hat. One that wants to hide the face and not allow the eyes to see. A hat to hide the shame, a hat to hide the guilt. Or is it a hat to hide the pain?

This hat is different from the other hats. It does not want to be chosen; it does not want to be worn. It wants to stay nestled on the bedroom shelf, completely wrapped in soft pink tissue paper, this hat is too scared to be loved, yet wants to be cocooned and enveloped in warmth. Not the harshness of reality. This hat is scared of the elements of life, the hat pin that will pierce and tear its heart, the rain that will lash down like shock waves on its surface. The hat almost wants to look like all the other hats and be neutral and blend and fade.

Yet, somewhere, within the depths of that hat is a flicker. A small yellow ribbon prepared to be seen, it peeps out beneath the darkness, a small light in the cold air. The wisp of ribbon tugs out and looks around almost rebellious. Feeling brave, the yellow ribbon edges out a little more and wraps around the hat so it can be seen by the world. This hat is now slowly glowing, a gentle glow, a timid glow but it's there. The hat is visible. The elements are now appearing. The hat pin is stabbing, the rain is lashing, and the hat is wobbling all over the place. For a while the hat doesn't know if it will survive the storm threatening to expose its fibres and carry it off in a tidal wave of fear. And then, suddenly, it recedes. The wind calms, the moisture dries, the pin stops piercing and the hat has made the journey against all odds. The hat feels a little less heavy, its yellow ribbon a little bit brighter, but still just a simple black hat.

GROWTH

When did it start, how did I know

The time when I felt I had started to grow?

My voice was so quiet, as soft as can be,

Weighed down from the trauma carried in me.

But a sound from the waves saying hello,

Here is the place for me to let go.

At first I stood back unsure of my fears,

Whether the clouds could fit all my tears

To wash away a lifetime of pain

And watch as it dances away in the rain.

Instead of the rage that tears me apart,

There's now room for peace to fill up my heart.

The ocean has opened the door to my mind,

To wash through the sadness and leave it behind.

The scars of my war might always be there,

But my bravery shines and will help me repair.

I am a warrior for all I've survived

My fight from within has kept me alive

I stand in the light not willing to hide

I no longer need battle the demons inside.

Open and ready to be the best that I can,

To truly accept the woman I am.

A HAZE OF MEMORIES

A haze of memories,

Easter egg treats all boxed up and ready to be unwrapped

Brightly coloured surprises too excited to wait more than time
offers

Looking at the row lined up, which one will get chosen?

The one that stands out the most,

All bold and red with the shiniest glittery paper

Or the small humble plain box on its own?

Simple yet special

Tiny but sweet

A discarded box honoured to be selected.

A haze of memories, a table laden with symbolic promise,

Scattered family around,

A picture-perfect image,

Broken edges carefully concealed between the laced material

Who will be the one to discover the true meaning of escape?

The youngest who asks the questions already written

Or the unspoken verse yet to be discovered?

A glass filled with sweetness or a cup swimming in salty tears?

A haze of memories,

A celebration of being free or an eternity of chains

Empty faces on silent chairs

Who will be the one to taste the offer on the table?

Paint a smile on a young mouth and swallow the fireworks
    within

Whisper the prayer beyond the shadow and watch the flock
    gather

Ready to rise up and flee the darkness.

A haze of memories,

Some to savour, ones to set free

The mist may not clear or sometimes seem real

But the echo inside keeps marching on to a painful beat

A house of cards waiting to fall, one by one,

Ready to be swept up and start again

Strong legs on young soldiers.

Who will join the gambling table?

A dice with no numbers or a chance to win

Who wants to select a haze of memories?

SURVIVING THE STORM

Blackened ashes crumble in a withered soul

Devoid of warmth and wrapped in stone

No forgiveness from the light of day

She sits there quietly and begins to pray.

There is no place that's left to go

In a barren land and all alone

Fragile and scared, she is so unsure

For reasons unknown, it's over once more.

Have the clouds taken pity as they unfold their wings

Or the rays taken space in the sky as they sing?

Maybe the ocean can slowly reform

From the strength of the waves

From surviving the storm.

SWEEP IT UNDER THE CARPET

Deny all you want, deny if you must, sweep away all the layers
of invisible dust

Pretend it's not true, pretend it's a lie, keep it locked up inside
from the naked eye

Sleep through the night, hide away from the day, it's easier to
ignore if it's not on display

Blinded by pride or blinded by shame, where will the fingers
point to in blame?

Were you aware, would you tell if you knew, or does fear cloud
the thoughts of what he might do?

Try and stay quiet, keep acting bland, why should you care if
they don't understand?

Who will you favour, when will you choose, why can't you
notice all that you'd lose?

The damage is done, you've left it too late, to ever be different,
it's now filled with hate

Consumed by protecting his secret once more, you failed yet
again to open that door

No wish to speak out, hide the dirt before found, remove all
the stains that tarnish the ground

Your silence speaks volumes, it echoes in you, but remember
these words, remember what's true

The dust won't stay hidden, it will come back and fight, to tell the world what has happened each day and each night

Keep sweeping his legacy under the stairs, for what's etched in the heart will never leave there

DECLUTTERING COBWEBS

Decluttering cobwebs is so hard to do
Layers of dust waiting for you
It's difficult to know where you should start
What could be found when you pull things apart
For in the midst of tumbling shelves
Are ghosts of memories kept to themselves
Shadows from photos not seen in a while
Echoes of sadness scattered in piles.

Decluttering cobwebs is so hard to do
Entangled in fibres woven like glue
One book stands out amongst all the rest
A favourite from childhood and one you know best
It's tattered and torn from hands over time
Beloved and treasured memories of mine
A chance to read through, beginning to end
Familiar words, from an old friend.

Decluttering cobwebs is so hard to do
Be lost in the moment, it's there just for you

Close your eyes for a minute, capture it all

A fascinated child, a face so enthralled

Not just from the stories of adventures told

But listening to how the endings unfold.

In a way, the picture painted is sad

It's one precious moment with her father she had,

For a short frozen minute, she had forgotten the pain

By listening to him reading, again and again.

Eventually the book was closed and let go

Discarded and forgotten, no longer on show

Until now it has chosen today to appear

Huddled together with others in fear

The books whisper quietly, which one will she keep?

Are we no longer worthy, meant for the scrap heap?

The well-loved worn books kept for so long

Sit back on the shelf where they belong.

Decluttering cobwebs is so hard to do

But in the delicate strands, a light has shone through

It glistens as threads unravel at last

One treasured moment from memories past.

A HOUSE OF DOORS

The house had a creepy feel to it. Covered with cobwebs and dark places where things could hide. An empty living room, devoid of heat in a house chilled from within. Many layers needed to cocoon a blanket of warmth to wrap the soul. The eeriest place was the basement. Dim lights and stone-cold floors. Lots of nails, planks of wood and workman tools lay scattered around. It was not a place to visit and she shuddered with fearful anticipation standing inside the door and could not wait to get out of the darkness. A hallway just as terrifying., with a street door looming inwards with strange scary strangers standing behind, waiting to pounce. When the key turned in the door or the bell rang, there would be a flip flop inside and a breath held until it was safe to let it go. Who knows what trouble would occur depending on which door was opened first?

A POCKETFUL OF CLOUDS

A pocketful of clouds, a safe space to breathe

A chance to pretend, a place just for me

I can sleep on the pillows, all wrapped up in love

Holding onto to a pocketful of clouds is enough.

I'm close to the stars that glitter at night,

Their magical sparkle, my guiding light.

The moon has two faces, one loving and warm

The other looks out for the eye of the storm

It speaks of the sound that tiptoes so still.

Tie your heart with a ribbon until it can heal

The whisper of trees who gather so high

Nurturing me on their path when I'm ready to fly

Let the wind spin around and capture the rain

That pours from your soul, in distress from the pain.

Dance in the rainbow, all colourful and proud,

Be beautiful and free in a pocketful of clouds.

NIGHT TIME

Plain wooden furniture adorned the bedroom. Stark doors that led nowhere. Stillness filled the air as she tried to stop breathing and play dead. She didn't want to be awake when he walked in. Her eyes kept staring at the solid wardrobe. Its darkness offering no comfort or shadow to hide under. As she lay there in bed, her ears strained for the sound of footsteps. Her heart was pounding and too scared to turn around, her hands gripped onto the nightdress pulling it over her knees. Clutching her teddy, she really wanted to sleep, but kept hearing a squeak from his slippers that was coming nearer to the bed.

Trying her best not to listen, she could hear the belt unbuckle slowly and the zip noise of the trousers. Praying that he wouldn't see her, she hid under the covers with her teddy and didn't turn until she heard the bed move. Slowly and carefully, she uncurled herself and knew he had gone to sleep this time. It seemed like ages before she could drift away. Everything echoed much louder in the dark, even the horrible clock that wouldn't shut up. Finally, she fell asleep with her arms tightly wrapped around her soft, cuddly teddy, waiting for night time to end.

AM I YOU?

I am blinded to what's in front of me. You are me but am I you? Standing there all alone, yet I've closed my heart to you. My eyes see red, the wall is so high, it's an impossible task to remove each brick one by one. My arms are scared to reach out and care. What does it mean to feel? Does it say I've forgiven you? Is it really your fault? Did I fail you for condemning you too? Is it wrong to hate you for what you represent to me, for what's on the surface surely can't be underneath?

My instinct to suffocate you with anger lies deep. My urge is to test you to see if you know how to show pain and reflect the reality that seems so unreal; it's like it didn't happen if I close my eyes. The mirror hides the truth staring back at me. It shows a blank reflection unable to register and accept the lost little girl looking back at me. Should I tunnel through the glass and take you with me, or leave you standing alone in the cold once again, waiting to be rescued? Can the door ever close once it's been opened? Will I know what to do? What if I can't love you? Am I strong enough to feel your pain? What happens if the ice refuses to melt around my heart? Will I ever be forgiven if I can't set you free? Will you in turn learn to love

me so I become you and join as two?

BIRTHDAYS

Two years ago today, you turned ninety two

That was the last time I spoke to you

I had one last chance to say goodbye

Knowing that soon you were going to die.

Your final birthday, one more card

I had no idea it would be this hard.

I hid my shame and nobody knew

Just how I felt still loving you.

The conflict and pain hit me each day

I really wish it would go away.

I'm so tormented from the memories inside

The ones of the truth are so tough to hide

There's so much of you still in my mind

So many memories, none of them kind.

And yet I wish you had reached ninety-four

So I can hear your voice just once more.

Because of all the things that made my life bad,

I thought, when you die, I'd be happy not sad.

It's hard to explain what I'm going through,

The loss of a dad I hardly knew.

You may have been here but never were able

To protect me from harm and keep my life stable

I grieve for what I deserve to have had

To know what it's like to be loved by my dad.

Who knows if you're listening to all that I say?

I cannot just sweep all the truth away

As hard as it is for me to move on

And deal with the fact you will always be gone.

But I'll still be your daughter, you will still be my dad

How can I miss what I've never had?

My heart splits in two when I think of this day,

Another year without you on your birthday.

BROKEN GLASS

Who wants to drink from a broken glass
Sordid and stained, left over and used,
Hidden in the depths of despair behind heavy doors?

Who wants to drink from a broken glass?
Wine cannot pour into fragmented shard
Ready to split the soul.

Who wants to drink from a broken glass?
Open the cupboard and pick something new
All shiny and bright, singing melodious tunes.

Who wants to drink from a broken glass?
Find the one not shattered in two
For it's too heavy a burden to carry ruptured pieces.

Who wants to drink from a broken glass?
Oh, the shame from displaying dirty wares,
Conceal the evidence, wipe away the signs.

Who wants to drink from a broken glass?

Too late, the damage is done,

Hold it up to the light and witness the flaws.

Who wants to drink from a broken glass?

No one will know if a sip is taken,

I won't tell if you don't.

IF ONLY THE EYES COULD SEE

I called your name. Every night I came to you, abandoned, lost,
a shadow looking for light. I'd sit by the window staring
out into emptiness, waiting for the moon and stars to lift
me out of the darkness.

You never heard my silent cry; you never saw my broken soul.
The glint of sharpness ignored as the wound got deeper;
the blood so deep within that only the right eyes could
see what others were blinded to.

Your hands never took mine. They wavered in their comfort.
You turned away and looked in the wrong direction. I
was left to climb the mountain on my own.

You could have lifted me over the ocean, not have to wade
through the deepness alone. I'd beg for forgiveness for a
sin that was never mine to take.

I stopped hoping for the eyes to see. I gave my heart but what
did you give me?

My scars, my wound, my battle, my journey to be free. I've
opened the gate to my path. Why don't you take my
hand and walk with me?

CINDERELLA

Standing wistfully by the light of the moon like Cinderella and her pumpkin, she waits for the magic to happen, so for one night she can forget who she is and dance in a different life. Her knight in shining armour, waiting to whisk her away on a sprinkle of stars, so her feet float like fairy dust on a bed of love.

Dashing and strong, his arms embrace her delicate fragility, never letting go. Gazing at her with tenderness, he sees the trembling of her soft mouth, the slight blush of excitement on her skin and the simple beauty of her dress. Not a handmaid's dress all plain and drab, but one of exquisite workmanship to be worn only by one deserving of its ownership.

For that moment she allows the light to come in and see her reflection in the dress; her hand gently hugging the soft woven fabric in amazement as the purity shines through. Spinning around, her heart feels light and free, like a dove discovering its wings for the first time. Captivated by the innocence of the dress, she wishes the night to keep the stars out longer and continue smiling upon her.

Her eyes tear away from her shadow and close. The clock ticking in the silence breaks the stillness of the night, daring to take the dream. Sleep little girl your time will come.

DARKNESS

The river no longer flows, the water runs dry

The sun has faded and all that's left is a barren stark emptiness

Darkness has descended

Cold and unforgiving, wrapping itself around like a tightly
coiled snake

No sound

No movement

No breath

Just still.

Watching, the figure hides behind the murky shadows,

Waiting for the moon to guide

A light to bestow on the path to safety, but it never comes.

No way out, no end in sight,

The figure sinks back into the shadows alone.

THE CAT

Night times were a blur of fuzziness and lots of shadows by doors. If the door opened it was scary. Who was behind it? If the door shut, what might happen? Yet she could only sleep with the door fully closed, as in a strange way, felt protected. One night, the door blew open in the wind and a cat found its way in, spending most of the night prowling around the bedroom looking for toys to play on the floor, keeping her awake for a night that would never end. The cat hunted as she quivered in her bed, too paralysed to close the door to the cat. Not once did the cat sleep or settle for warmth of a hug. She never wanted to invest her heart in a cat who received all the care and attention. Maybe she should have been a cat.

GHOSTS OF THE PAST

They say it is time to forgive and forget

When the dead are buried and the ground has been set

The bareness of stone, no flowers to show,

Is this really it? Is it time to let go?

Yet justice evades with you underground

Pervasive of action, no chance being found.

Who hears the plea in the wandering sky,

With the tree branches broken, clouds empty and dry?

For one voice has listened, that much is true.

The door is wide open, but it isn't for you,

The ghosts of the past drift on their way,

They are no longer needed in this present day.

IT'S ONLY A DRESS

Two girls, two different dresses, one pink and frilly, the other
plain and simple

A dress to be worn, a dress to be shown, a dress to be torn, a
dress to stay home

What if they swap, would the girls feel the same? After all, it's
only a dress

at the end of the day

Two girls, two different dresses, one shy and unsure, timid and
scared

A dress too dirty for some eyes to see, a dress should be
young, clean and carefree

Would the girls still be friends if they both wore the same?
After all it's only a dress

at the end of the day

Two girls, two different dresses, one sings out loud all happy
and silly

A dress so perfect and fits like a glove, a dress filled with

  pleasure, it's shining with love

Can one girl's outfit cause such sadness and pain? After all it's

  only a dress

at the end of the day

HEADLESS SOLDIERS

Headless soldiers marching to the sound of a soulful beat, a familiar journey each time with an endless destination. Is there any point stopping to pick up the wounded when they have fallen, as the same faces will still be there on return? One by one, they line up waiting to endure the perils of misfortune.

Headless soldiers fall like skittles as they all come undone, a silent crash through the enemy's door to fight each time in an unfair battle. Protect the armour from a wielded sword as the glint of sharpness tries its best to break through an unused shield. Pick the moments to be seen, for a war cannot last forever.

Headless soldiers, day by day face the hands of time which forgets to move. Sand trickles slowly in the dust of an empty land, without the promise of a new horizon. But the enemy will grow weary, the trickery soon to fail, as new strength has gathered among the wounded.

Headless soldiers, marching to the sound of a different drum, bravery not witnessed by a blind enemy who lacks the audacity to look forward. Now is the moment for the war to be won, as headless soldiers stand ready to fight. No weapons needed in a courageous heart, for the mighty will return home together as one.

I NEVER ASKED

I never asked why you didn't hear my fears when you thought
it was okay to strip the moon from the night sky and
take away its chance to shine

I never asked why you closed your shutters from the warmth of
the sun no matter how hard it tried to melt your heart

I never asked why you crushed the hand that dared to hold on
despite the pain which never unfroze

I never asked why you unwrapped the gift that was never
yours to own, time and time again, being broken

I never asked why you fed the bird who always waited for the
small crumbs to be thrown its way, even though it was
never enough

I never asked why you had the power to make time stop
moving with every breath you took, even though the
clouds still travelled

I never asked why your mouth barely spoke, yet your eyes told
a thousand stories

I never asked why you chose the wrong path with so many
signs pointing towards a better journey

I never asked why after all these years, what is the answer to
the question

Only now do I know why. I never dared to ask.

LITTLE BIRD

Little bird trapped inside its prison, encased within metal bars of a soulless cage not knowing when to move. The bird has only known one place to call home, even though it is a place filled with danger and uncertainty; the familiarity of the same acrid odour of sawdust and dry woodchips lined in its cage providing its only source of comfort where the bird goes to sleep.

But the time is approaching, for the safety net of four walls has crumbled leaving the key unturned to loosen the heavy chains anchored on the lock. A reluctant step and a gentle push from an unseen mothering hand encourages the bird to lift one tiny foot forward and then another. A small heart beats loudly in a tiny chest, unsure if the outside world can hear as it tentatively looks around, as if seeing daylight for the first time. To begin with, the light is too bright, dazzling the bird, for it is not ready to look into the light, but averts its gaze to the comfort of the shadows reflecting in the corner of the room.

The bird looks back with sadness, the fear of leaving its only home too scary to ponder over without knowing the consequence. Yet the overwhelming desire to nestle in a soft bed of dewy leaves and warm feathers fills the bird with bravery and very slowly, a beautiful wing opens out, followed by another. The flowery scent of sweetness brimming in the sunshine fills the air with intoxicating freshness as the little bird rises up into the air. Swooping with delight, the bird glides along the breeze of morning basking in the warmth of the sun's hazy glow, as it makes its way out into the wonders of freedom. Tiny beads of moisture trickle on its beak, only this time they are rain drops of happiness, shimmering in the horizon. The little bird allows the drops to continue falling until the whole sky is dancing with joy. Fly high little bird; find your dream in the colours of a new rainbow.

BEHIND A PERSON'S SMILE

No one knows what goes on behind a person's smile

It can sometimes seem hidden from the naked eye

Facing each day with perseverance and grace.

Being brave does not always have to be visible,

Inner strength can be quiet, yet dignified.

No one knows what goes on behind a person's smile

It's the unspoken word that can hold all the courage

An entity of years in silence and reserve

A day in the life of an unknown warrior

A voice so gentle, it deserves to be heard.

No one knows what goes on behind a person's smile

Walk a hundred miles in shoes so worn down

In amazement from footsteps that still carry on.

Dealt with cards from hands never asked to be chosen,

Destiny's path is not set in stone.

No one knows what goes on behind a person's smile

Not every gateway needs to be wide open to see.

Expand the horizons at a pace just for you

The journey uphill has plentiful rest stops,

A chance to discover a wonderous view.

NOTHING STAYS HIDDEN FOREVER

I never asked to be born in a web full of lies

With the sound of my voice kept hidden inside

No words yet spoken from fear to speak out

Trembling and quiet, too scared to shout.

How long will this last? I really don't know.

Please take me right now to a place you can't go,

In a land filled with magic, a safe space to fly

With fairies around me, who light up the sky.

How can I fight and be brave like I should

When I'm only so little, just trying to be good?

When is my time to take off the mask?

Oh, to feel safe, is all that I ask.

There's no way of knowing how long this will be

If the truth will stay hidden, just wait and you'll see,

One day this will end, your time will come

When the world crashes down and your life falls undone.

LOOK AT ME

I see your face, do you see mine?

A mouth that never flickers, the smile that never happens. Do
you see mine?

A mouth that tries to speak but has no words, a smile that is
hand-painted on.

I see your eyes but they do not tell, they do not speak.

The eyes that have no windows, no light, just empty shutters
on a windowless frame. Do you see mine?

The eyes that are wide, they are frozen in time. They fear the
light, for the eyes that reveal will no longer see.

I see your hands. The hands that show no mercy, the hands
that inflict the pain.

The hands that penetrate a wall that should never be broken.

Your hands are older. Your hands know better. Do you see
mine?

The hands that are young, the hands that are soft. These
hands should hug, these hands should hold.

These hands have imprints that will never leave. Hands that try and wash away the truth but never feel clean.

Hands that are forced into battle yet too exhausted to fight back. Hands that should be attached but instead are detached.

I see your body. Do you see mine?

The one that lies in wait, like a tiger about to pounce. The one that lies so still like a mouse caught in a trap.

What do you see now? I see my face, do you see mine?

The mouth that speaks, the mouth that sings, the smile you no longer own.

I see my eyes, do you see mine?

The eyes that show the truth, the eyes that allow the light to come in and see the soul.

I see my hands, do you see mine?

The hands that hug, the hands that hold. The hands that will now fight and re-attach.

I see my body, do you see mine?

The one that moves, the one that expresses, the body that now spins its own web and traps but no longer is caught.

Your life has ebbed but mine still flows. Yours has no hope, mine still has a chance. A chance to see and a chance to be seen.

I see my life, do you see yours?

SHH LITTLE GIRL

Shh little girl, don't make a sound

I can't keep you safe if you are found.

Shh little girl, don't show your tears

I'm not strong enough to hold all your fears.

Shh little girl, please lay still

I'm sorry I took you against your will.

Shh little girl, it's come to an end

I'm sorry for being such a bad friend.

Shh little girl, please hold me tight

I promise everything will be alright.

Shh little girl, all tiny and broken

I can lay you down like you've never been woken.

Shh little girl, please go to sleep

I pray for your soul or the angels will weep.

Shh little girl, please take your flight

I will stay behind and continue your fight.

Shh little girl, you can now fly away

I have given you wings for a brand new day.

LOVE

Looking through the frosted glass, her eyes could see a little girl sitting by the Christmas tree. All shiny and sparkly with wonder on her face as she shares the joy being with her family. The outsider wanted to be in that place, to experience safety and warmth within the house. This is what the world should see. That's how love is meant to be.

One cuddle, one hug, to be held, soothed and rocked, not abandoned, ridiculed or mocked. Not hated or smacked and made to feel sad, for the one outside only knows what it's like to be forgotten. Her childhood has gone, she knows no joy, it's always the same. But to live in a life free from pain. That's how love is meant to be.

To have soft hands that brush and play with her hair and show her with words, she is cherished, and special, all open and caring. Not secretive and shameful and made to feel scary. Maybe a time will come when truth can be shared and a heart open wide to take in new memories and feel good inside. That's how love is meant to be.

SEARCHING

Where are you, are you there?

Did your soul get snatched before it had a chance to start over

All new and wiped clean, or has it shattered into a million
pieces like my heart?

Sharpened edges cutting into the sky

No place yet to go but gathering in readiness to light up the
night.

Where are you, are you there?

Are you an echo in the shadows that grips my hand dragging
me through the same story as I fight my way out of the
storm?

I look for solace in the clouds as they gather me up in a warm,
gentle breeze to guide me forward along the way.

Where are you, are you there?

Can I hear you in the trees, whispering and conspiring to hold
me hostage as I stand underneath an umbrella of fading
leaves?

Soon winter will come and strip your cover

No longer so powerful or dominating, now naked and bare for the world to see

My body pushes with all its might to set myself free from the entangled branches

I continue forward on my journey.

Where are you, are you there?

Are you the mist of the ocean hiding in my salty tears or have you fallen amongst grace against the wrath of perilous cold waves, as they sweep you further away from me?

My feet plant firmly in the sand as I stand bravely in my true form at the water's edge, looking out onto the gateway of freedom

One day I will join the ocean to meet the waves and say hello when they have forgiven the storm

Until then I leave behind my tired, heavy stones

They no longer need to be carried

As I walk away, a residue of footprints stay imprinted in time as it waits there for my return

SECOND HAND GOODS

Crumpled and discarded, abandoned into a dejected heap like unwanted rubbish. No second thought for the one tossed aside. Used goods, stained and ripped with no reason to unwrap any layers and be warm.

Who even cares if the brown paper withers? It has nothing to give, no reason to keep fresh. Who has time to notice if someone else takes the wrapping and peels it off layer by layer? Rough hands on a smooth surface. Suffocated by string, worn out and frayed trying to keep the goods tightly bound up. Loose ends make it easy to unravel and see what's underneath.

Show no mercy for the one no one knows, the name has no purpose. Untie the coils and pull apart the edges. It doesn't matter if they split, for a replacement can easily be found just around the corner. Bright red paper, ready and waiting for the party to be over.

Who will worry if the layer has broken? Erase the blot on the landscape, it's too much trouble to keep the twisted threads, for they are not wanted. Smooth hands on a damaged surface. No longer needed, so tether and bind the wrapping, still crumpled and torn.

Who will see if it's second hand goods? Maybe a stranger will take pity and adorn new layers, wrapped up and bright with ribbon, a rainbow of colour disguising the sorrow.

Who will remember except the one who knows what it is like to be left out in the rain with only the most modest of covering, sheltering from the storm. Underneath, the shiny coating will always have the desire to be accepted as new and be cherished by smooth hands on a smooth surface. One person's second hand goods, another person's treasure.

SILHOUETTE OF A SONGBIRD

A creaky wooden floor where hints of unspoken promise have stood. The shadow of silent walls darkened in anticipation of being spoken to. One chair sitting patiently, the wooden legs resting on a scratched surface. A faceless audience watches and waits.

Solid footsteps follow an anxious heart. Eyes glance quickly, absorbing the empty colour. Ears take in the gentle tapping of hands dancing on a line ready to take flight. Muscles pull tight, eager to compress the voice within and stay hidden.

But the match lights and colour flickers from the silhouette standing still. Soaring up to the echoes above, a sound emerges bursting free from a cage like a captive volcano on a lonely mountain. Go beyond the stars and cross the ocean. Let the voice carry over the darkness and carve out a different name in a new light. A realm of non-existent ribbon dance at the feet of the figure that sways and moves round, with only a hint of breath shuddering in a sleepless soul.

A jubilant songbird flourishes its wings like never before, as it listens to the beat of approval from a roaring drum. Solid footsteps follow a joyful heart, open to the warmth of sunlight pouring in on a once-blackened canvas. Empty of picture, now filled with room to paint a cherished dream.

TAMING THE WAVES

Only when you stop and breathe for a minute
Do you realise how far you have come.
To swim through the storm with the tide against you
Is a remarkable feat, so bravely done.

It's humble and courageous, facing fears of the wild
When you can't always see the sand from the shore.
Taming the waves are no longer required,
It's time to embrace the ocean once more.

The sky won't forget the rain in the clouds
If it ceases to flow every day.
A rainbow of colour needs no permission
If it wishes to highlight, sometimes in grey.

Heaven can wait for the jewel in the crown,
When the mermaid is ready to bask in the sun.
A beautiful sparkle in the essence of light,
A chance to make wishes, be free and have fun.

TAKE MY HAND

Take my hand child and walk this way, I will be your guide on
your journey today

Put down your stones that are stacked so tall, let me shoulder
the weight, I won't let you fall

My arms will protect you from all of your fears and give you
the strength to let go of your tears

May the river flow to cleanse you within; I will always be with
you when you begin

Your heart is so lost, it's hidden in cloud; please know I am
near child, it needs to be found

My footprints go with you in love and in pain, to help you find
your path to regain

My hand will not waiver, I hold you so dear, my love for you
child will always be here

Lift up your eyes and look to the sky, you've always had
courage to take off and fly

No longer fear darkness and look to the light, just know I'll be
with you each day and each night

Let your heart bleed no longer, put down the knife. We will do
this together and build a new life

Your heart might feel broken and unsure to feel, but I know
you are brave, I have faith you will heal

You will not be alone when you walk through that door, I will
be waiting to talk to you more

Take my hand dear child and walk this way and alongside each
other, you will guide me today

BLACK AND WHITE STORIES

It is easy to recite the same lines in a monotone voice of black and white. No need for a dress rehearsal from an unchanged show. Only when words gain colour from a different writer does it resonate deep inside. Who knew if this is what the story was about? Were blinkers on so tight, it could not take in the picture? Perhaps not. Maybe what is right in front of the naked eye is too dark to see without lenses from another angle. Time stands patiently, waiting for a new chapter to be ready.

THE BEAST

The river runs red, old leaves wither.

Naked and cold, she soon starts to shiver.

How did she get to be so far from home,

Lost in the woods, all on her own?

Where is the wolf?

He is nowhere in sight.

Did she imagine the beast in the night?

The moon would not lie, its brightness so pure.

Illuminating stars guide her some more,

Cautiously walking through crystals of snow

She continues her journey with no place to go.

But lights up ahead ignite into warmth

Giving the strength for her legs to go forth.

When in front of her lies the beast she had slain,

Crackling in fire, covered in stains.

The wolf is no longer a dream in her head,

It's safe to return from the life she has fled,

In a world full of colour, once filled with grey,

For a new dawn awaits, now the beast is at bay.

THE BUTTERFLY

Darting between the shadows, she moved softly, trying not to break the silence of the night. She knew sooner or later he would find her, but for now she was safe.

The moon seemed sharper tonight. Edges defined the uneven glow as if to say, you can do this. I can be your sword and shield. But she didn't always trust the moon. Its guidance often failed to protect the reflection that wanted to shine.

But this night felt different. She had seen the light urging her to come out and play. Be a butterfly, spread your wings and dance in the sky where no one can reach your heart. The light refused to flicker, it stood steadfast and strong to encourage her to emerge. With trepidation she edged forward and held out her arms, one by one feeling only the gentle breeze warming her skin. It felt soft and kind. A new sensation she had never experienced, it almost made her feel giddy with excitement.

Swaying with the wind she spun around, her breath inhaling the sweet aroma of freedom, no longer shuddering from the intoxicating smell of fear. In the stillness she could hear the music in her heart beating within, trying to escape the entity of silence.

One by one the stars came out to watch her. Only their eyes could see her innocence meant for no other. She did not want the night sky to betray her, for she knew her time was brief. The flicker of light signalling it was time to be still, she floated back down. The stars gathered, forming a link around her heart, keeping it safe until the butterfly was ready to be set free.

THE CAR

How can a blue car, a toy just so small

Carry so much meaning for me at all?

It's the one gift I remember you gave to me.

I would play in the hall in the hope you would see

But you didn't watch when I tried to show

How fast this shiny blue car could go.

It's almost like I wasted your day

To spend some time and see me play.

I took the snippets of memories we shared

And told myself that you really cared.

Maybe I wasn't the perfect child,

You never allowed me to run or go wild,

For anything shown was seen as a sin.

So, I tried to suppress any laughter within,

It was hard to be quiet and ever so good,

But sometimes my noise was misunderstood,

My chatter and talking, I tried for a while

To see if I ever could get you to smile.

It worked on occasion, but a laugh never came,

I kept wondering why I felt so much shame

To only experience that one half of you,

The other side, nobody knew.

Until now, when I realise what you have done

It's too late for me, you are already gone.

I can no longer look at the car with such joy

When deep down I know it was only a toy.

THE DOOR

A different door, the same key,

A chance to escape, a place just for me.

What's there to see on the other side

No longer in shadows having to hide?

Peaceful and calm, everything still,

No pain from my body, no longer am ill.

Gentle and warm, the sound from the sea

Lovingly wrapping its waves around me.

Take all the stones tearing your heart,

Lighten your load and throw them apart.

One by one, large stones and small,

Chuck them away once and for all.

The key can be turned if you want to go home,

Just remember I'm here, you're never alone.

This place can be found through the door in your mind,

Come back to me, don't stay behind.

This is your door, solid and steady

It will open and close when you are ready,

The world is so tough especially right now

There's a survivor in you that will get through somehow

No matter in life who has the key,

You have the power to set yourself free.

THE FORBIDDEN FOREST

Stillness, no sound to be heard. Trees stop whispering, dark
leaves close, pulling sharp thorns upright. A hidden barrier for
only small eyes to see

Birds hesitate to fly; wings stay close in anticipation of a
    sudden release

Clouds shift together trying to block any glimpse of light
    invading, while dark eyes gleam in the shadow,
    menacing and fierce

A small heart pounds in a tiny body, rocked in fear, the
    forbidden forest is not a place for a little girl lost. Bare
    feet lift gingerly, testing branches to keep their silence

Snap. A frenzy of wings rise in the air as big hands lunge and
    grab the little girl. A silent scream from a trembling
    mouth, the haunted face from her nightly dreams

Scream all you want little girl, for no one shall hear your cries
    deep in the forest

Do not hurt me, do not try. I have done no wrong, I promise I
    won't cry

Hands pull on ragged material, roughness of skin chafing on a young body, blood falling, falling, falling

Fingers delve further in; strike the knife on a shielded surface

Do not hide little girl, I shall always find you deep within and rip your secret from your soul

No, you will not take my secret; I am the keeper of my soul. It is mine and only I shall bear my soul for I will rise from the ashes and be the warrior

Stand away from my path. I am the stronger, not you. You are no longer welcome in the door of my dreams

The axe wields glinting and sharp, crashing down on the wolf disguised in sheep's clothing. Throw open the curtain of the forbidden forest so truth can prevail and find a way out

Little lost girl, go on with your journey to an enchanted forest all ready and waiting, no longer be frozen, no longer be small. Throw the wolf to the devil once and for all

THE ICE QUEEN

Darkness is all around, with shadows in her head, the absence of light from her heart

The empty cold chill as the solid shield of ice creates an unbreakable wall around her body

The axe is there trying to enter, but unable to shatter through the shard of glass

Nothing can penetrate the ice queen. Yet the ball of red fire still burns her hands, the pain so intense it has all but consumed her

The demons inside the wall are stronger than the ones exhaled out in her breath

They torment and torture, mock and shame

The flames that try to melt the ice only hold her hostage for longer

The power of the axe of darkness so strong, it blinds within

The fury rampages, threatening all that lies in its way, for she shall seek and she will destroy

There is no escape for anyone

The ice queen exhales and the red mist clears

Walls of fear implode but a small fragment of ice finds its way
out and becomes a tiny drop, clearing a path for when
time unfreezes

THE OCEAN'S VOICE

Sometimes you just have to listen quietly to the ocean and let
it speak to you

A voice for today, a guide for tomorrow

Silence speaks volumes in the roar of a wave

As the salty air cleanses the spirit, clarity opens the doorway of
kindness

A zigzag path to an unfamiliar territory

One where the mind dares to drink from the water's edge

And unlocks the gateway to a new tomorrow

It's not without fear as you step into the ocean's tide to ride on
a storm

But the cup will replenish a thirsty soul when the ocean is there
to steer the way

A kiss of a promise for a new horizon

Where hearts gather to dance under the light of an enchanted
sunset

Go with grace and heal from the warmth of the ocean as it
wraps your body with love,

Carried over to safer shores

THE PIGEON

She would do her best to catch them and watch as they flew off with panic. That was the fun part, until one day, one was finally caught. She was not sure if she had meant to kill it. She did not know. It all happened so quickly. There was a sudden urge in her that wanted to hurt the pigeon and did not know why. Suddenly, it stopped beating its wings and knew she had jumped on it in anger. She could not even look at the bird. Part of her felt glad it was dead and wanted the pigeon to suffer and feel pain, but part of her felt really scared when she noticed the blood around her. She stood frozen on the spot, bracing for the hands to smack, but without saying one word it was picked up with a tissue and thrown in the nearby canal, and just walked away.

THE STORM

Perilous waves thrashing on chalky stones, leaving no escape, not even the smallest ones daring to show. The cascade of water mercilessly stripping the stones of any hint of rebellious colour, no longer standing out amongst the others.

The thunderous storm lashes down on frenzied stones, for they shall be found by the eye of the beast. Exposed and laid bare of the gritty sand, nature has taken off the elements cloaked in disguise.

The stones are now grey, all huddled together, cold and unfamiliar, on a stark barren ground. Jagged and broken, no longer so brave, the hand of fear ready to strike.

The stones are not worthy to stay by the shore; the wind howls and flings them back to the depths of despair. The beast that lies low shall venture and seek a lifetime of chains and anchors deep, for the cold callous stones awaiting their suffering.

Cast off the net that weighs down your heart and swim away little fish, to a sea full of smiles. Your journey no longer blinded by stones, the ocean is yours to explore and discover. Shine little fish, glitter and swim, bask in the golden rays of warmth by day and let the moonlit sky guide your way by night. For the storm has now passed, the waters have calmed, swim little fish to a brand new day.

THE WEB

Shimmering in the darkness, the dewy net tries to reel in the outsiders who are blinded to its presence. Unable to see itself, it needs others to shine a light on the web hiding in the shadows and entice it out of the depths of invisibility.

The woven web so tightly spun, it tangles the eyes to see beyond. So many layers to unravel, it intertwines and devours the mind. Too many dangers present themselves to break the chains that anchor it down. Too scared to climb below, it sits and waits for prey to come.

The peril of attaching itself beyond the elements of where it sits alone and safe weakens the strength of its long silky web. For the beauty of the eye should not be in the beholder, but be encapsulated by its own ray of light. It should glisten in the sun and not wait for the moon to be its guide.

Too many distractions confuse the unspoken silence. The web is delicate and fragile. Nature tries its best to break the silver lines that blur the boundaries. For it is not the web that is hunted, but wants to be the one who is captured. Safe and nestled within another web, where it can be wrapped around with softer layers.

THIS IS REALITY

Tighten the noose on a silent scream; this is reality and not just
a dream

The hangman of terror strikes her with fear when the sounds
of his footsteps are all she can hear

Where can she hide? There is no escape, when the predator
comes to catch her awake

Shivering and shaking, her eyes wide with fright, she knows he
will win with her body tonight

Go under the covers and stay still in the bed, his hands might
be kinder if he thinks she is dead

Dry tears falling, sharp like a knife as she waits for the hands to
ruin her life

Each squeak of the slipper, the tear of a zip, the smell of the
leather torn from his hip

The clock has now stopped, it's frozen in time as she curls up
her legs and closes her mind

Heaviness looms on the weight of her flower as the force of his
hands wield all the power

Her nightdress no longer shields her humility, cold and unable to protect the fragility

Her bed is now damp, a towel pats it dry, she is too scared to turn and look into his eye

What would she see if her mind made her peep, a man with two faces etched in her sleep?

One painted picture she loves with her heart, the other so twisted it fractures apart

Tick tock, tick tock, shake the clock hands to go, he's done with her body it's now time to go

Pull up the blanket and silently pray, to keep her surviving another long day

WAITING

Waiting, every day is a waiting game. Waiting for morning to begin, waiting for night to end. Just waiting

Waiting to be watched, waiting to be invisible. Waiting to be seen, waiting to hide away

Waiting for footsteps, waiting for silence. Waiting for the pattern of the wallpaper to disappear

Waiting for the moon to shine so dreams can come. Waiting to fly up into the sky of a different world. A world where there is no more waiting

TIME TO GO

Empty, missing, gone. A space no longer taken by you

An invisible chair still waiting for the seat to be filled, but it
remains bare. Frayed cushions from a worn out body
that could no longer wait around anymore

Time to go.

Yet the cobwebs linger. Echoes of a distant voice shadow each
room, each space, every corner

A faceless memory behind the door with a blanket to keep the
cold out

A hesitant greeting each time, unsure to say hello or goodbye.
The same wish to continue the sentence and then
remember you're not there

Time to go.

A kettle to boil but nothing to pour. No use for tears to
replenish a dry cup

The white hollow shell with no reason to be there but still
hovers within your hand, clasping both sides

Eyes stare at the cup, taking in the stark whiteness now devoid
of its warmth and colour

A secret desire to drink from the same well and remember
each drop. But the water has ceased to flow

Time to go.

Tired steps lift a heavy soul. Up the stairs on a creaky path to
your room and back down

Thinly covered skin on a withered hand, clutched out
fragments of paper now discarded

Once dotted with your own messages distinct with long
strokes and sharp lines

A flurry of numbers collected as a trophy with names

My name

Still wanted but no longer needed

Time to go.

Half a house with layers removed. The dust not yet sure where
to settle, still trying to find a place to feel at ease

A hesitant step around each piece searching for the sound, a
familiar existence of breath wanting to locate a non-
existent soul

Now devoid of movement

Time to go.

Ring on your door, but you will not answer. An absent stranger
in the same house. Different words hover to make new sounds

Silence is louder in a lonely shell with no cover to keep warm

Picture-framed stories speak of different endings with happy
faces in the dreams on show

Yet unspoken tales stay behind within the patterned walls and
dance away from the light keeping the ever-present
darkness from escaping, but too painful to say goodbye
to the invisible space

Each moment, each ending

Every one just as hard as the next

Time to go.

UGLY DRESS

Pretty with flowers, liberating and free
Lots of movement for the eye to see
A little girl's dream to wear such a dress,
But under the layers she cries in distress.

All severed and torn, damaged and shaken
For her childhood innocence has now been taken
No longer simple and worn in vain,
She now tries to hide to cover the shame.

Like an animal trapped, she starts feeling wild
For she is no longer just an unblemished child
The dress is now dark, full of anger and sin,
She hates the dress and what lies within.

Her voice in her head is shouting and screaming
To wake up her hands and stop them from dreaming
Struggling to hold back expressing the rage
From what she is feeling at such a young age.

Her hands are sore and ready to fight

They can no longer stay down frozen in flight,

A little girl lost and unsure of her life

She lunges forward to pick up the knife.

She rips at her dress, the one she holds dear

She no longer wants to be covered in fear

The knife slashes through, all split and cut open

Little girl standing all naked and broken

She has nowhere to run and nowhere to hide

The guilty feelings still crying inside.

Now, go hateful dress and leave her alone

For this child is no longer yours to own

Set her free ugly dress, once and for all,

For Cinderella shall go to the ball.

WHY?

Why dare to hope when it's only a dream?

Why look up when there only is down?

Why imagine colour when there only is black?

Why change paths when there is only one road?

Why have a voice when it's only a whisper?

Why bother sharing when there's only just one?

Why ask for more when nothing is left?

Why have a heart when it's only a shadow?

Why give it water when you can't shed a tear?

Why try to answer when there's never a question?

Why try to finish when there's never a start?

Why fix the cracks when it's always been broken?

Why begin when there's only one ending?

EMPOWERMENT

Little girl so still, no longer be small, your time has come to rise
and be tall

It's safe to unlock the key to your voice, now is the moment to
sing and rejoice

Take all your strength shining inside and share with the world
the bravery you hide

We stand as one and together unite, to face the world and
take on our right

As women we know we were meant to be, to believe in
ourselves and set our minds free

SANDS OF TIME

No salt left to taste on an unquenched mouth, dry from the Sahara sun. A clock ticks loud from a beating heart in the quiet terrain, guilty for breaking the silence. Who will make the first sound? The serpent, as it glides like silk across the desert sand, or a scuttle in the shadows, of a creature unknown to man? The mind plays tricks, blinded by scorching rays, as footprints go swiftly through the land. Not even an imprint left behind as the earth swallows up and captures the trail. Surely a horizon will be found in an arid, hostile world, an escape off a fearful path. Not even a swirl of cloud to push the breeze through quicker.

But in the distance over the dusty terrain, a hint of green, lush and rich, full of unspoken promise. A place yet to be discovered. A journey full of wonder of what could be, perhaps a drop from the tears of a cloud waiting to release the moisture, a brave bird claps its wing in anticipation of a voice to a silent drum. A destination with only one way forward. No looking back on an unchosen path. Take the comfort from an unseen hand and forge a new sound in the way ahead. Determined footsteps will carry through, strong and fearless.

Sands of time tick softly in a warm heart. Be kind and gentle, let the gates open wide and soar up above like a guide of an angel destined for the sky.

JOURNEY OF HOPE

From the time I was young, my world was quite scary

Unable to predict what the eyes could not see

A perpetual feeling of unease and shame

The constant reminder battling in me.

I couldn't shake off the aftermath of guilt

From the merciless hands that my body endured

It was my fault I said, I never fought back

I only went through what I thought was deserved.

At night time I'd look to the moon from my window

And silently call to the light in the sky,

I held my hands together in prayer

And ask up above, to please let me die.

I never heard any answer inside,

I thought he had abandoned me, left me to cope,

But night after night, I'd continue to stay

And somehow managed to never lose hope.

One day at a time, one week to a year

I survived through the eye of the storm

But for what I'd endured, I wasn't too sure

If this is how relationships are meant to form.

I'd sell my body to the devil if asked

If I thought it was love I could get,

But somehow my needs remained unfulfilled

It was not the best way to try and forget.

Fast forward some years when I was a mother,

I knew I had to change course

To break the cycle from the chains of abuse,

A mind filled with shame and remorse.

I chose to speak out against all the odds

After the silence of so many years,

By reporting their actions to the police,

My choice, but one filled with such fear.

What would now happen to the accused

For speaking out in such a way?

But I knew I couldn't continue to live

If I didn't take action this day.

In the first time in ages, I was believed,

The police had given me hope,

It helped to stop the trail of destruction

A gradual journey on a continual slope.

Life carried on, the accused never charged

For he had run away to far away shores,

But something had changed inside of me,

I had confidence, something not seen before.

How did this happen, I ask myself?

I was never permitted to have my own voice.

It's something I strive to aim for each day

By giving myself the power of choice.

With perseverance, tears, counselling and faith

I carried on in my journey of hope,

I found strength learning drama and started to sing,

A rainbow at the end of a kaleidoscope.

Where am I now in my journey of hope?

In a better place I thought I'd never be in,

Knowing deep down inside, I'm worth so much more,

For I'm not the one who has committed the sin.

Never give up, your strength is your beauty,

Even though it sometimes feels locked up inside.

Each woman deserves a chance to be heard,

Together as one we will no longer hide.

It has been a struggle, that part is true,

Not knowing at times if I wanted to live,

But with the ocean walking beside me through storms,

My journey of hope has much more to give.

TIME TO RECLAIM

No more hiding

No more shame

It's my body now

Time to reclaim.

You had no right

To take what was mine

I will not allow

What you did to define.

I am powerful

I am strong

I will let the world know

What you did was wrong.

Women like me

Are now here to stay

To prove our worth

We'll not go away.

You may have run

Far from my sight

I will never give up

What I believe is my right.

I have the voice

You own the sin

I set myself free

From my fight within.

In all my young years

When you gave me pain

No longer I'll shudder

When I hear your name.

I will not go quiet

It's time to be loud

My faith gives me strength

To make myself proud.

I share my life story

To give courage and hope

For all those brave women

Who struggle to cope.

I know you will heal

Take hold of my hand

I'm here on your journey

Together we stand.